I0481980

Make Money from Home

How to Make Money Online and Escape the 9-5 Rat Race

LELA GIBSON

Copyright © 2017 Lela Gibson

All rights reserved.

CONTENTS

Introduction

I want to thank you and congratulate you for buying the book, *"Make Money from Home"*.

This book has actionable information on how to make money online and escape the 9-5 rat race.

If I only had one thing to tell anyone out there who is either new to the job market or is graduating, that would thing would be:

"Jobs suck! Well, at least the old-fashioned version of a job where you have to do something you don't really like from 9-5 and are simply paid for your time to only slave yourself on the job." I like calling this the 'sell your time' personal business model where you literally exchange your time for money. In other words, you sell your time to someone and they pay you for it.

That's not right. If you've been there, and actually experienced what I'm talking about, you'll know that this *personal business model* actually sucks. I'd say you need to do things differently; work in your PJs or underwear, avoid the commute, respond to emails from a hammock as you sip coffee, and so on.

I'm sure you've heard the benefits of working from home—and yes, they are all true. As you read this book, you will discover some things that will surprise you about what it's truly like when you don't have to wake up early to beat the traffic snarl up.

Besides that, and primarily, this book will teach you the many different ways of making money from home to escape the 9-5 rat race, and be able to do many more things you love.

Thanks again for buying this book. I hope you enjoy it!

Copyright 2017 by Lela Gibson - All rights reserved.

This document is geared towards providing exact and reliable information in regards to the topic and issue covered. The publication is sold with the idea that the publisher is not required to render accounting, officially permitted, or otherwise, qualified services. If advice is necessary, legal or professional, a practiced individual in the profession should be ordered.

- From a Declaration of Principles which was accepted and approved equally by a Committee of the American Bar Association and a Committee of Publishers and Associations.

In no way is it legal to reproduce, duplicate, or transmit any part of this document in either electronic means or in printed format. Recording of this publication is strictly prohibited and any storage of this document is not allowed unless with written permission from the publisher. All rights reserved.

The information provided herein is stated to be truthful and consistent, in that any liability, in terms of inattention or otherwise, by any usage or abuse of any policies, processes, or directions contained within is the solitary and utter responsibility of the recipient reader. Under no circumstances will any legal responsibility or blame be held against the publisher for any reparation, damages, or monetary loss due to the information herein, either directly or indirectly.

Respective authors own all copyrights not held by the publisher.

The information herein is offered for informational purposes solely, and is universal as so. The presentation of the information is without contract or any type of guarantee assurance.

The trademarks that are used are without any consent, and the publication of the trademark is without permission or backing by the trademark owner. All trademarks and brands within this book are for clarifying purposes only and are the owned by the owners themselves, not affiliated with this document.

Before we get to a point of discussing the specific ways through which you can make money online, we'll start by outlining the benefits of working from home so that feel motivated enough to implement what you learn from this book.

Working From Home: Why It Is Such A Great Idea

The benefits of working from home are simply endless. Nonetheless, we'll briefly go through a few of them. The main benefits, if you ask me, include the following:

1. You choose and manage your own schedule

Today, most of the work done remotely is on a flexible schedule. For instance, if you're a content creator or a web developer; you can almost certainly do your writing or coding any time it suits you provided you meet deadlines. Therefore, if you're a night owl, you can rejoice! With this kind of control, you can put in your eight hours without necessarily beginning at 8 in the morning.

Do you like working at specific hours? Well, by working from home, you'll still have time for a personal break to do anything you want. Even if you only have ten minutes, you can do something that wouldn't otherwise be possible (or thinkable) in a traditional office: take a refreshing power nap, bust a couple of samba moves, listen to a few sax tunes, or even play your guitar! You are certain to return to work feeling a lot more refreshed than you would after ten minutes at a desk browsing the internet.

2. You save money

Without a doubt, when you don't need to bear all those commuting costs, you'll see an instant change in your bank account. You'll also see savings in other places; for instance, you will no longer have to force yourself into formal suits and polished shoes if that is really not your style. It also means you will no longer have different wardrobes (for your job and for the rest of your life). You will also save on food costs because if you work from home, you will be in a position to whip up your own coffee and lunch instead of buying them from the local cafe.

3. If you have a team, you can have enjoyable and very effective meetings

I bet you can't give me a single name of anyone who likes meetings (even the free coffee and donuts can't beat the dreary, stuffy conference room, and the pen-clicking sales guy). By working remotely, you not only get to choose your breakfast and seat, you also tend to be a lot more effective. With only a couple of clicks, you can have fifteen people on a video call that probably lasts ten minutes instead of thirty—and you can use the video call's chat function to share documents quickly (forget creating copies or having everybody search their emails) or in adding all the critical comments without interrupting anyone.

4. You'll have the opportunity to learn more and become more independent

Working from home means you don't have any colleagues a couple feet away from you or a tech team one floor up. This means you automatically find yourself developing the skill of seeking answers for your tech related problems and becoming more active in finding what you need all by yourself. While you can still get help or ask questions when you need to, most of the time, you'll find yourself going the extra mile of checking out your company's wiki, doing a

Google search, or even downloading a free guide to find your answers.

Moreover, working from home also means you'll end up learning new essential skills because you really need them to work contentedly remotely. For instance, you'll probably realize that the development of the ability to write more concise and clear emails, and sensitivity to the different schedules of your team (if you have any) out of necessity.

5. You can fashion an office out of anything and locate it anywhere

Working from home does not mean you have to get some clunky desk that takes up a corner of your living room, an ugly office chair, and a large monitor. How you set up your home office is a personal choice; you can fit your office anywhere it fits your life. One of my friends who is a remote worker conveniently uses his kitchen breakfast bar as a standing desk (imagine all those health benefits and zero investment). One of my other friends fashioned a section of her bedroom closet into some kind of a 'hidden' office so that at the end of the day, she just shuts her work away!

In case you're wondering, you're not tied to your home either and it doesn't mean that the only other option is the coffee shop around the corner. You can comfortably do your job while travelling, having fun in the great outdoors, or even while enjoying your favorite orchestra at a live concert. All you might need is your laptop (or a smartphone) and an active internet connection.

IMPORTANT NOTE:

Many people consider working remotely and working as a freelancer to be the same thing. This is not right. Having a remote full time job means that an organization or company has employed you but you don't have to be at the office physically. You may note the use of other terms such as telecommuting, home-based working, or virtual working to describe this type of job.

On the other hand, a freelance job simply refers to when you work for someone else without any formal employment obligations. This type of work is often project based and ends with the completion of the job.

While both types don't require you to wake up every morning and report to an office (thus being home-based), this book notes that they are different. I have equally considered both of them in the book, in case you decide to take up either.

Now that you know the benefits of working from home, I know there's another lingering concern that affects just about anyone before they leave their 9-5 jobs to become freelance workers, or remote workers. That concern is how to start, or rather, how to transition from formal employment to home-based employment.

Let's talk about that so that you can smoothly leap into the freelance life with minimal apprehension.

How to Transition From the 9-5 to Home-based Work: A Primer for (mainly) Freelance Workers

It seems that more and more people are kissing all the lifeless cubicles and stuffy work environments goodbye and opting for the freelance lifestyle where they can become their own bosses, or just to work remotely and be in control of their schedules and most of their work. Actually, Forbes reported that today, about a third of workers in the US consider themselves as freelancers. Indeed, a major shift is happening in the workforce.

If you've been thinking of jumping on the bandwagon yourself, or perhaps you've been longing for that day when you can bid your boss goodbye, walk out, and never look back, you're not alone. However, if that is the case, it means that you are perhaps like most people who although want to become freelancers, there's always something keeping them from actually doing so. That thing is fear and uncertainty.

Without a doubt, strolling out of that secure 9-5 job and rolling the dice as an inexperienced freelancer can indeed be enough to have you quivering in your boots. Nevertheless, as most people have discovered, it's definitely and surely doable. If you're wondering 'how', there's something you ought to know, something that will help you successfully transition from your regular 9-5 into a freelance life:

1. Don't forget to check your contract

If you can start building your freelance business while still at the comfort of your steady paycheck, that's awesome! Nonetheless, you cannot afford to skip this important step.

A number of companies have stipulations in their employment contracts that essentially prevent their employees from taking on work from outside that could be competitive with their own business in a way. Therefore, before you try growing your side hustle, you should try combing through your contract again to ensure you are not going to ruffle any feathers.

If you have a difficult time trying to wade your way through all the legal gobbledygook, you can set up an appointment with HR. The important thing here is to be well-informed beforehand.

2. Begin early

Unless you have stacks and stacks of cash stored in your attic, there's no way you're going to be able to make a seamless leap from your present job without any kind of prior planning. Regardless of what your ambitions and dreams, you still need a means by which to pay all your bills and meet all your basic needs.

This means you have to start building your freelance career before jumping ship from your 9-5; you have to build what many would call a side hustle. You can start taking on some projects you can complete over the weekends or after work—this means you should not try working on these during your normal working hours—so that you can start growing a client base and establish your brand as a freelancer early.

As you will realize, this will most likely translate into spending long nights and weekends in front of your computer screen. Cumbersome as it may seem or be, it is worth the effort and is what it'll take to begin building a robust foundation from which you can grow your home-based business.

3. Explore your options and take the leap

Regardless of how well prepared you actually are, the truth is that taking the final leap from your full time job to a freelance career can be gruesomely scary. If preparing as we've discussed so far still fails to take out the fear over the idea of taking the leap, perhaps it is important to take a bit more time so as to explore all the options before you can take the leap.

Maybe your current employer will let you take a part-time role. With this working arrangement, you'll still be able to get your paycheck while also having time that you can use to work on your own business; perhaps your employer is the kind type that would love to be your first customer as a freelancer.

If all the above are not viable options: the terms of employment are against you, your employer will hear none of it, and things like that, you can also decide to save enough money first so that when you leave, you can sustain yourself for a given (projected) period of time.

What I mean is you never really know. You should thus not try to count anything out; ensure you are considering all possibilities. Perhaps it's what will make all the difference in the long run.

Gradually, you will get to a point where you no longer have the time to commit yourself adequately to the regular job and freelance projects. While that can turn out to be stressful, this is actually a pretty good sign, as it basically means you have put together up a steady enough foundation and can now transition from your regular job without necessarily having to worry about the sheer panic.

Thus, when you largely feel ready (even though, fair warning, you may never feel completely ready to make the leap), it is now time to make the move and begin your new life as a freelancer or home-based worker. From personal experience, I can tell you that while jumping ship is indeed frightening; it's also amazingly exhilarating!

Don't forget to have fun in the process. You earned it!

4. Network

You probably already have a good understanding of the significance of networking; regardless, now that we're here, I will drive the point home.

When you're just beginning your freelance business, some of your greatest assets will be the people you have in your web of contacts. They might either have some work for you or have the capacity and chance to link you up with other professionals who could gain from your services.

Therefore, you need to get out there as early as possible, attend networking events, seminars, and conferences whenever you can. Join the industry-relevant associations. Set up informational interviews and meetings with businesses and people that interest you. Send tailored LinkedIn notes or even an announcement saying something like "I am freelancing" to a number of your existing contacts. Just place yourself out there; these connections will soon pay dividends as you build your freelance business.

Now that we have the preliminaries out of the way, let's discuss some of the most profitable work-from-home opportunities available to you:

The Best Active and Passive Work-from-Home Jobs to Target

In case you're not sure which freelance and remote jobs to start off with, here are several recommendations segmented into active and passive home-based work ideas:

Home-Based Active Income Work Ideas

By active income, what we mean is that these jobs, although home-based, require that you trade your time for revenue. These jobs are much like a 9-5 job in that if you stop working, you stop earning. The main difference is that instead of commuting to an office, you can complete these jobs from home. Most people start here, as this can help them accumulate enough money to grow a passive income business.

In this respect, some great active-income options (from a work-from-home perspective) include:

Transcriptionist

This job generally pays $25 an hour or even more. I would recommend this job if you're looking for a flexible job that doesn't require any prior experience or very little when it does.

Transcription simply entails you listening to some audio files and typing everything that is being said. Since the job is relatively easy, companies are hiring transcriptionists that have no much experience and therefore, you'll find a number of job postings only asking you to have a computer (and internet connection) to begin. Transcription jobs usually vary from a doctor's medical dictation to a college lecture, and many companies will allow you to create your own schedule.

How to Snag a Job in This Field

If you're just getting started, here are some leads on where to find transcription jobs even as a complete beginner:

Quicktate.com

TranscribeMe.com

TranscribeAnywhere.com

You have to note that before someone hires you, most employers will give you a short test to help them measure your attention to detail and typing accuracy before hiring you for any official tasks.

Website Tester

This job generally pays about $10 to $15 for every test taken.

Many companies are paying online website testers to ensure their websites are intuitive as well as easy to navigate. As a website tester, you essentially follow the instructions offered to you to check out a website. An average test will take about fifteen minutes. If you choose this option, you should consider registering with up to twelve different companies because the opportunities to test these sites are on a first-come-first-serve basis. In case you're wondering, some freelance website testers earn up to $2000 per month.

How to Snag a Job in This Field

Start with the sites listed below. Make sure to register with many different companies for chances to test as many websites as you can.

Userlytics.com

UserTesting.com

YouEye.com

When you get into the system, you will get emails when companies require testers, and if you are the first one to respond, you should expect to take about 15 to 20 minutes to finish the test. Most sites will need you to have a webcam and/or a microphone, which you don't need to worry about anyway because they're built into most laptops. Tester sites usually pay through PayPal within one or two weeks.

Virtual Assistant

This job generally pays around $10 to $15 per hour. I would say this is the perfect job for you if you're extremely organized and great at multitasking.

Today, many companies are hiring self-employed virtual assistants to save on employment costs. As a virtual assistant, you complete typical office duties such as managing calendars, replying emails, data entry, and helping with social media management from your house.

How to Snag a Job in This Field

If you're in this type of work, you can scrutinize platforms such as the ones below to find virtual assisting opportunities.

FlexJobs.com

Upwork.com

PeoplePerHour.com

Corporate English Trainer

This job pays about $15 per hour.

If you're a native English speaker, have basic computer skills, an interest in other cultures, and love chatting over the phone or online, this might be the perfect job for you. You will find the office experience very helpful because most students work in a corporate environment anyway. This job also requires you to have a computer and an excellent internet connection. Being bilingual is automatically a plus.

Many students in countries like Korea, Japan, Germany, and France who are looking for English speakers to help them learn spoken English by way of conversation. The sessions will focus on things like running a meeting or making professional small talk (as a trainer, you'll get details on how to teach every topic, and you'll also receive 2-day training prior to starting the job).

The lessons themselves will happen on a live internet video service such as Skype or over the phone, and since the students you'll be working with are in different time zones, you should expect to work at night sometimes.

Each week, you can expect to work for a minimum of 20 hours and a maximum of 35 hours.

How to Snag a Job in This Field

You can begin with GoFluent.com, an English training company that works with 12 of the biggest corporations in the world. You can also find a job for an ESL (English as a second language) teacher—these are more structured. Just visit iSpeakUSpeak.com (ISUS) which is a placement and training company.

Survey Taker

This job generally pays between $1 and $50 for every survey completed but depends on the amount of time required to complete the survey.

This job may require you to fill out an opinion poll, answer questions concerning shopping habits, or even review a particular product and then you get paid in cash (mailed directly or via PayPal), or with points you can redeem for gift cards.

How to Snag a Job in This Field

Simply visit platforms such the ones listed below then sign up with the sites available (as many as you can). These platforms will contact you when surveys fitting your demographic pop up; you can then take them immediately and earn the reward.

PaidViewpoint.com
DarwinsData.com
PineconeResearch.com

TIP: Do not register on any platform that asks for a membership fee or that requests your bank info or social security number. Any site that is vague about payment should also not be an option.

Direct Salesperson

Generally, the amount you will receive as payment for this type of job depends on the company; however, the typical payout is about 20% to 35% of sales in terms of commissions. If, therefore, you have an entrepreneurial spirit, a lot of energy, and love talking to new people, this job is probably the best fit.

To understand exactly what it is, you can think of Mary Kay or Avon: you get to organize family get-togethers for instance to sell the wares of a company whether they're gardening supplies, bath products, wine or books. With time, you create a base of customers.

How to Snag a Job in This Field

You can apply to the companies directly; these companies may include the following:

Stella & Dot: This jewelry company has been generating over $100 million sales each year.

Pampered Chef (deals with kitchenware)

The Cocoa Exchange (specializes in chocolates and more)

Avon (cosmetics)

You can also go to the Direct Selling Association website here DirectSelling411.org where all the companies listed accept to adhere to a set code of ethics so that they are only offering legitimate opportunities. Typically, reps make a little investment to begin, which is legitimate and standard, and may sometimes have to pay a fee for the goods sold.

Once done with that, you can now work as little or much as you want, and generate revenue according to how much you sell.

Other active income opportunities include the following:

• **Writing:** You can find writing jobs from Upwork.com, Freelancer.com, Fiverr.com, TextBroker.com, Problogger job board, etc. Keep in mind that there are many forms of writing; you could be a ghostwriter (where you write ebooks), blog writer, web content writer, SEO writer, Academic writer etc. You can learn more about where to find writing jobs here[1] and here[2].

---

[1] https://realwaystoearnmoneyonline.com/money-earning-directory/writing/

[2] https://www.dreamhomebasedwork.com/the-best-upfront-pay-online-writing-websites/

- **Web development and design:** If you can design and develop apps, websites, plugins, book covers, logos etc., you can get paid for that. You can find these jobs on Upwork.com, Freelancer.com, Fiverr.com, 99designs.com, Guru.com etc.

- **Voiceovers:** If you have a good voice as well as access to recording equipment, you could do voiceovers for pay. You can source voice over gigs from Fiverr.com, Upwork.com or Freelancer.com.

Next, we will discuss passive income ideas.

Home-Based Passive Income Work Ideas

By passive income, what we mean is that these work-from-home ideas require an initial amount of active input but after they're set up, continue to generate revenue with minimal active input. If you're looking for complete financial freedom, home-based passive income ideas are your best choice. In this regard, you can try:

Publish eBooks

Today, the eBook industry is a booming business with approximately 1,064,000 eBooks downloaded per day on Kindle (Amazon's popular book platform). Even the tiniest slice of this pie can add up to an impressive passive income every month.

The best part is that a properly written eBook does not take much energy, time, or effort and you can actually write a non-fictional eBook in less than 2 weeks—if you're really passionate about it and very driven. As a self-published author, you can also succeed from writing novellas, short stories, and other works of fiction.

If you have nurtured the desire to share some bit of wisdom to the world, or get your short story out to the public, go for it.

You, however, need to appreciate that the best way to begin is writing about the stuff you love and really know about. Your passion and enthusiasm will present itself in the way you write and your readers will actually handsomely reward you through giving positive reviews. Keep in mind that reviews are very important in driving sales as far as publishing is concerned; the more, the better.

To learn more about making money with eBooks publishing, read this.[3]

Affiliate Marketing

Affiliate marketing is the process of promoting other people's products or services on your websites for a commission of every sale made. Your job here is to partner with affiliate programs, obtain their affiliate links, and promote them to your following.

---

[3] https://bullshit.ist/how-i-make-400-a-month-in-passive-income-by-self-publishing-68fa948edff5

The following are some of the available affiliate networks to consider joining:

ShareAsale: With more than 3,900 affiliate programs spanning forty categories, ShareAsale is indeed one of the largest affiliate networks today. ShareAsale offers reversal rates, earnings per click, average sales amount, and average commission.

Amazon Associates: Amazon associates makes sure you earn from the products you advertise as well as the qualifying purchases. In addition, they have competitive conversion rates that are sure to help you maximize your earnings.

Clickbank Clickbank is undoubtedly the place to start if you're a new affiliate marketer because it typically lacks the common stresses common with more advanced affiliate networks.

Click on any link above to get started.

DropShipping

In a dropshipping model, you create a simple website and sell a particular product in a specific niche. Once you sell the product, you then contact the supplier and purchase the product, and the supplier will then ship the product to your customer directly.

Dropshipping is a very interesting area you should consider learning. Please visit the links below to do so:

To understand how dropshipping works, please visit this page.[4]

To know how to make money from dropshipping from home, read this.[5]

Photography

Do you consider yourself some kind of a shutterbug and see photography as one of your hobbies? If so, you can turn that into a passive income stream by selling some of your greatest snaps for cash.

The demand for royalty-free images is on the rise and many sites of stock photos will readily accept fresh submissions from professional as well as amateur photographers. While

---

[4] https://www.shopify.com/guides/dropshipping/understanding-dropshipping

[5] https://realpassiveincomeideas.com/make-money-ecommerce-drop-shipping/

you definitely have to meet particular set requirements first, if you've got some great images in your portfolio that you don't mind parting with, you could use the stock photo sites to generate a steady source of passive income. For more information about that, please read this article.[6]

Let's take a look at some of the best apps you could use in this regard.

Foap

Foap is a great app that's currently available on Android and iOS. With this app, you can directly upload your pictures to the app and offer them to the global marketplace for sale. All photos have a $10 price tag and when one of your shots sells, Foap takes $5 and you get the other $5. The real money comes when the shot sells multiple times—often amounting to hundreds of dollars.

Clashot

Clashot is another app you can use to turn your cell phone into a photobank. The only thing you have to do is upload your pictures, then sit back and see the sales roll in. On

---

[6] https://www.theworkathomewoman.com/selling-photos/

average, you should expect to get fifty cents up to $80 worth of commissions from a picture you submit.

Filming and Posting 'How To' Videos

This can earn you between $1 and $2 for every 1,000 hits; the payment depends on the number of people clicking on the video.

Have people ever asked you about your secret to learning the piano in a week, or how you repaired that dead phone? That right there is an opportunity to make money. We all know how to do something or have a hobby we enjoy; if we decide to, we could turn such knowledge or passion into profits through YouTube.

Just sign up for a free YouTube account, buy a digital camera, or use your phone to record yourself demonstrating and explaining how to work your magic. If you're more tech savvy or have an enthusiastic filmmaker as a friend, you can utilize desktop software like Windows Movie Maker to make a slicker video.

As you upload the video to YouTube, sign up with its partner program. YouTube will then use your video to display advertisements by placing them in the video and you'll generate money from the advertisements themselves, click-throughs and video views. The important thing here is to place a unique spin on your video especially when you realize there are many other videos on the same topic.

How to get started

Once you shoot the video, say with your phone, open the YouTube application and press 'send.' If you're uploading it from your computer, just go to the YouTube website and upload by clicking the 'upload' button at the screen's upper right corner. You will see an area to drag your video file.

To enroll for the partner program, go to YouTube settings and check the circle right beside 'allow advertisements'. Now click on 'view additional features' and opt in on the YouTube monetization page. Generally, before you receive payment, you should earn a specified minimum; you also need to know that YouTube only pays monthly. In case you don't earn enough in a particular month, the balance automatically rolls over.

Take On Design Work

If you're a creative, you need to think about putting your creations up for sale by taking advantage of the marketplace platforms in existence today. Actually, these platforms will handle everything from physical products, payments, to the customer service. In the end, you worry a lot less and put your focus on creating because you don't get to keep inventory on hand or deal with the daily operations.

Here are various examples of such platforms:

Redbubble

As an independent artist on Redbubble, you can apply your designs to dozens of products ranging from t-shirts to coffee mugs. The company then deals with the manufacturing and shipping of these products for you. Moreover, they offer flexible options regarding pricing to give you the opportunity to determine how much passive income you generate from every item sold on the platform.

The site currently hosts more than 350,000 designers, artists, and creators who are selling their work passively on the site; and you can join them today. In any case, the process of signing up is easy and free.

Zazzle

You can also use Zazzle to place your art for sale on autopilot. You can set up shop here by signing up, picking a name for your store, and start creating.

You can place your designs on numerous products; some of the most popular items include iPhone cases, T-shirts, invitations, shoes, shower curtains, and many other options.

Like Redbubble, Zazzle will take care of the manufacturing, shipping, as well as customer service for you. With a unique program called Name Your Royalty, Zazzle also gives you full control of your passive income earnings.

Invest in Index Funds

Index funds are forms of mutual funds that contain a portfolio made to match or track the market index components like the S & P 500 (standard and poor's 500). Index funds are very useful especially as long-term investments because they can return up to 7-10 percent of your investment. This means that if you put in a million, you get up to $100,000 each year. If you are not very familiar with real estate but still want to make real money, this is perfect for you as it simply entails setting up with your bank and forgetting it such that you allow it to grow.

When it comes to index funds, I would recommend Dollar Cost Averaging, which is purchasing a fixed dollar amount of a specific investment on a regular basis. Each month, without trying to look at your paycheck, you set it up and it pulls cash from your paycheck automatically. It then invests it on your behalf so that you never have to see your cash— and if you can't see money in your bank account, you obviously will not be tempted to spend it.

A good place to start with index fund investing is betterment.com- be sure to check them out to learn more. You can also visit this page to get the finer details about index funding.

You could also create apps, which you publish on different app stores, you can create online courses, which you sell online, start a blog, have a membership website etc.

Conclusion

Thank you again for buying this book!

I hope this book was able to help you to give advice how to make money online.

With the many options you can choose from, tying yourself to a 9-5 job is no longer an option. The ideas we've discussed in this book are just the tip of the iceberg; if you do more research, you'll unearth many more active and passive incomes ways to make money from home.

My last piece of advice is very simple: please actualize as many methods of making money from home as you can before you eventually decide to settle for a few, stable ones. This will help minimize the risk and maximize your earnings.

The next step is to take action.

If you found the book valuable, can you recommend it to others? One way to do that is to post a review on Amazon.

Please leave a review for this book on Amazon!

Thank you and good luck!

Preview of 'Freedom: How to Make Money Online and Become Financially Free by Creating Passive Income'

Before you can learn the specifics of building a passive income, it is critical that you understand what you are venturing into so that you don't start with a wrong idea of what it is you are working towards as well as what to expect from your efforts. Let's begin.

Passive Income: A Comprehensive Background

A passive income, also called a residual income, is simply the money you earn when you are not actively working. If you are actively working, it means you will receive some money (active income), which, when you stop working, you stop earning. With contract work or active work, you have to do some work to receive pay. In other words, you MUST exchange your time (hours, minutes, days, weeks or even months) for pay. In that case, if you are not working, you cannot be paid; it is simple logic!

This is always not the case with a passive income. With passive incomes, you earn whether you work actively or not. To create a passive income stream, you will have to put in some work upfront to get the ball rolling. You will however get to a point where your income stream will become passive such that it generates revenue on its own without you having to work for it. Think of publishing a book on Amazon for instance. After doing the upfront work of writing and promoting the book in its initial stages, you will get to a point whereby the book can continue making money whether you do anything to promote it or not. That's passive income!

Before we head any further, we have to discuss some things about a passive income because these things are important and will help you understand the nature of a passive income. Some of these include:

1: *Passive incomes are often not permanent incomes:* Get it right: some online passive incomes may last for years, decades, or even centuries. They can however never be permanent. This is because all forms of income eventually dry up at a given point for one reason or another.

2: *It is not a one-time lump sum payment:* Some incomes such as inheritance, sale of assets like pieces of land, or sale of stocks are one-time lump sum payments. This is not the case with passive income since a passive income is a source of income that has a sense of continuity over a certain period.

3: *Some passive incomes are semi-passive:* You may be your own boss but you will need to do some work (even if its management), although you will not receive pay for maintaining your investment.

For instance, if you build a house and rent it out, you will definitely receive your passive income from the tenants but when they move out, you will have to invest some energy, money, and time to maintain the vacated premise and seek other tenants.

4: *Passive income streams need maintenance:* Whether it is checking emails or paying taxes on your passive income, you have to do some of these activities for maintenance since they keep your source of passive income going.

5: *Your passive income might be another person's active Income:* No matter what kind of online business you invest in, you will have to hire people to do some work that help you earn your passive income. In other words, your passive income builds on leveraging on other people's active income to succeed! For example, if you have a freelance writing marketplace for instance, you will have to hire some people who will be writing or editing your articles. You will have to pay them hence they will receive active income but their work is what shall help you earn a passive income.

Now that we have established these critical things about passive income streams, the next thing we have to consider is why the internet is the best way to create multiple passive income streams.

Check out the rest of Freedom: How to Make Money Online and Become Financially Free by Creating Passive Income on Amazon.

Or go to: http://amzn.to/2nTo8oC

Check Out My Other Books

Below you'll find some of my other popular books that are popular on Amazon and Kindle as well. Simply search for these titles on the Amazon website to find them. Alternatively, you can visit my author page on Amazon to see other work done by me.

Ketogenic Cookbook: Quick Low Calorie Ketogenic Crockpot Recipes with 7 Days Meal Plan

Freedom: How to Make Money Online and Become Financially Free by Creating Passive Income

Mediterranean Diet: Instant Pot Cookbook with Delicious Recipes

Alice the Superbug

Madison and Astrid's first magical journey

Intermittent Fasting: The Essential Beginners Guide for Women for Weight Loss

Chakra Healing: Chakra Healing and Karmic Awareness for Beginners

SEO 2017 for Growth: The Ultimate Guide to Learn Search Engine Optimization with Internet Marketing Tips

Psychology: How to Analyze People Using Human Psychological Techniques, Body Language Signals, Social Skills and Personality Types

Paleo Smoothies: Recipes to Energize and for Ultimate Health and Weight Loss

Belly Diet Smoothies: Delicious Smoothie Recipes to Flatten Your Belly, Improve Your Gut & Burn Fat

Keto Diet: Keto Diet Guide Cookbook for Beginners with Meal Plan and Simple, Delicious Recipes to Lose Weight and Look Good

Online Business from Scratch: The 9 Step Guide to Building a Profitable and Sustainable Online Business

Weight Loss: 20 Easy And Fast Diet Tips For Losing Weight - An Easy-To-Follow Weight Loss Guide

Ketogenic Cookbook: Ketogenic Cookbook for Beginners with 7 Days Meal Plan

Negative Calorie Diet: Cookbook & Guide Which Will Help You To Burn Body Fat, Lose Weight And Live Healthy

Negative Calorie Diet with Anti-Inflammatory Diet Guide

Make Money Online To Achieve Freedom

Negative Calorie Diet with Smart Fat Guide

Negative Calorie Diet & Clean Eating: Cookbook & Guide Which Will Help You To Burn Body Fat, Lose Weight And Live Healthy

Smart Fat: Cookbook with Fat Meals Which Help You to Lose Weight, Get Healthy and Improve Brain Function

Anti-Inflammatory Diet Guide: The Guide to Reduce Inflammation and Live a Healthy Life Without Pain

Essential Oils: The Young Living Book Guide of Natural Remedies for Beginners for Pets, For Dogs

Clean Eating: Cookbook and Guide to Restore Your Body's Natural Balance and Eat Healthy

Anti-Inflammatory Diet Guide: The Guide to Reduce Inflammation and Live a Healthy Life Without Pain

Dash Diet: Cookbook for Weight Loss with Action Plan and Easy Recipes

Air Fryer Cookbook: Quick, Healthy and Easy Low Carb Air Fryer Recipes

Psychology & Habits Of Highly Effective People Box Set

Leptin Resistance: Leptin Diet to Control Your Hormones, Get Permanent Weight Loss, Cure Obesity and Live Healthy

Negative Calorie Diet & Dash Diet Box Set

Negative Calorie Diet & Weight Loss Box Set

Habits of Highly Effective People: What Are the Habits of Successful People?

Slow Cooker: Cookbook with Slow Cooker Recipes

Weight Loss Cookbook: Meal Prep Cookbook for Weight Loss and Clean Eating

Weight Loss Cookbook: Mediterranean Diet for Lasting Weight Loss

Negative Calorie Diet & Dash Diet Box Set

Slow Cooker & Instant Pot Box Set

Children Books: Madison and Astrid's first magical journey & Alice the Superbug Box Set

Belly Diet: The Zero Belly Diet Step-By-Step Guide Which Helps You to Lose Your Belly and Enjoy Your Flat Belly

Weight Loss: 20 Easy and Fast Diet Tips for Losing Weight - An Easy-To-Follow Weight Loss Guide

Instant Pot: Instant Pot Pressure Cooker Cookbook with Easy and Healthy Recipes

Vegan Cookbook: Vegan Cookbook For Beginners, For Kids And For Teens For Diabetics With Pictures

Low Carb: Low Carb Diet Cookbook with Low Carb Keto Recipes for Batch Cooking

Ketogenic Cooking: Ketogenic Cooking With Your Instant

Pot

Passive Income: Passive Income Tutorial with 7 Online Ideas to Generate Passive Income Streams for Beginners

Low Carb Diet: Low Carb Diet Recipes Cookbook for Beginners for Batch Cooking

Make Money From Home: How to Make Money Online and Escape The 9-5 Rat Race

Bonus: Subscribe To The Free Enhance Your Business Report!

When you subscribe to Freedom Destination via email, you will get free access to a report. All you have to do is enter your email address to get instant access.

This report is going to discuss 10 important, and possible crucial facts/ideas that if implemented, will increase your business as well as your profits.

You can access it here: http://bit.ly/2tXwgKQ

www.ingramcontent.com/pod-product-compliance
Lightning Source LLC
Chambersburg PA
CBHW071242220526
45468CB00002B/966